Totem
Tsartlip
Bay

Salal &
Forget-me-not

Wild Rose

Pacific Dogwood
- Provincial Flower

Cariar Park

VANCOUVER IS A GARDEN

Mock Orange

Vancouver is a Garden
Donna McClement

McCLELLAND AND STEWART

To my best friend
my husband Steve

ACKNOWLEDGEMENTS

I am deeply grateful to the many people who have helped to make this book possible. In particular, I would like to thank Mark Stanton for his assistance in the initial stages of the project and Heide and Egon Otten for their much appreciated support. My gratitude is also extended to Massot Nurseries for their valuable information.
Above all, special thanks to my husband, Steve McShane, for his kind assistance, unfaltering optimism and good humour throughout the preparation of this book.

Published in Canada by McClelland and Stewart Limited
The Canadian Publishers
25 Hollinger Road
Toronto, Ontario M4B 3G2

© Donna McClement 1985

Canadian Cataloguing in Publication Data
McCLEMENT, DONNA
   VANCOUVER IS A GARDEN

ISBN 0 7710 5435 1

1. Gardens – British Columbia – Vancouver.
2. Flowers – British Columbia – Vancouver.
3. Vancouver (B.C.) – Description. I. Title.

FC3847.37.M22 1985 917.11'33 C85 – 098095 – X
F1089.5.V22M22 1985

Devised and Produced by David Bateman Ltd.
58 Townsend Court, Buderim 4556, Qld. Australia

Typeset in 12/14 Baskerville
Printed and bound in Hong Kong by Colorcraft Ltd.

Introduction

Everyone has their own unique view and feeling about Vancouver. Some will see it as the vitality of the downtown business district; some as its mountains, vast ocean, or the majestic silence of Stanley Park; whilst others might paint a picture of the lively activity of Chinatown, the quiet elegance of Shaughnessy Heights, the old-world atmosphere of Granville Public Market or the serenity of Nitobe Garden.

The varying descriptions might give the impression of a seemingly incongruous city, but with its abundant lush foliage and flowers – it is a beautifully integrated, if moody, city. Shady trees canopy Kitsilano's streets, suspended flower baskets sway from lamp posts in historic Gastown, and flowers throughout the city spill

(continued overleaf)

Horseshoe Bay

Mountain
Laurel

Japanese
Azaleas

Nitobe Garden

out of tubs, cascade over balconies, and crawl along fences. Dotted everywhere are lovely parks and beautiful public gardens. Even in the hectic downtown district tree lined streets and beds of flowers are all carefully tended.

Each season colours Vancouver with its own inspiring beauty – the delicate pastels of early spring with its cherry blossoms, magnolias and dogwoods; the warm hues of summer. The vibrancy of autumn is seen in the reds and burnt orange of sumac and dahlias; lastly, the subdued evergreens of our gentle winter.

In this book I have tried to capture those images which reflect Vancouver as I see it – a vibrant city amidst flowers in a magnificent setting.

Donna Mc Clement

Salal

'Shirofugen'

'Kwanzan'

From early March into May, Vancouver is a carpet of delicate pink and white petals from Japanese flowering cherry and plum trees. One of the first trees to blossom, I am told, is at English Bay not far from this charming bandstand in Alexandra Park. Built in 1914, the bandstand's remarkable scroll brackets complement the delicacy of the blossoms.

Higan Cherry

'Shirotae'

Plum

Japanese Cherry & Plum

9

Vancouver Art Gallery

The Vancouver Art Gallery is one of our cultural centres.
A sandstone and granite structure, it was built in 1910 to
house the provincial law courts. In 1983 it was converted
for use as the Art Gallery, although the building is still
often referred to as the "old Court House".

Daffodils, one of the most popular spring bulbs, were
growing in front of the Gallery when I visited in April.

Daffodils

Detail of Gallery

Magnolia

Law Courts

While the old Court House marks Vancouver's solid
heritage, the new Law Courts mirror its modern
image. With a sloping skylight and seven tiers of
plantlife, the building resembles a giant
greenhouse.

Flanked by the old Court House to the North and new
Law Courts to the south is Robson Square. As well as
being a centre for lectures, concerts and other cultural
events, this award-winning complex charms visitors with
its cascading waterfalls and outdoor cafes.
Azaleas, pansies and other spring flowers were in bloom in
Robson Square but I was particularly drawn to the
beautiful magnolia tree.

Robson Square

Robsonstrasse

soft pink buds

brownish-orange
centre -- use
Burnt Sienna

deep yellow
-- use New
Gamboge

hairy leaves
& stem

azure
(also rose-pink)

Forget-me-not

14

The Manhattan Courtyard

On the north side of Robson Street are the Manhattan Apartments, one of the earliest apartment buildings in the city. The graceful entranceway leading to Manhattan Courtyard, below the Apartments, is a mass of hanging flowers and potted plants.

Robsonstrasse is a delightful section of Robson Square with a distinctly continental flavour. The European-style delicatessens, cafes and charming courtyards entice passers-by to browse or stop for a bite to eat.

Just minutes from the heart of the city is
Stanley Park. In this 400 hectare forest
grow immense Douglas fir, cedar, hemlock,
and the famous Hollow Tree which is large
enough to hold a car. At the feet of these giants
are lush ferns, buttercups, wild berries and other
wild flowers.

Hollow Tree

Surrounding Stanley Park is the famous seawall which protects the shore from erosion and provides a scenic walkway. Along the route is Siwash Rock. Indian legend claims that this natural rock formation is a monument to the unselfishness of a mythical Indian hero.

Siwash Rock ?
Seawall Promenade

When I was there in mid-June, large stands of Yellow Flags were growing by the water's edge of Lost Lagoon. Although the lagoon is now landlocked, at one time it would "disappear" when the tide receded –hence its name. The lagoon is a refuge for numerous migratory birds and waterfowl.

Yellow Flag

18

Two of Stanley Park's major attractions are the
Vancouver Public Aquarium and Stanley Park
Zoo. A free standing sculptured Killer Whale
was recently erected in front of the
Aquarium where several of these mammals
now live. Nearby, a beautiful square shades
zoo visitors during sunny June days.

Stanley Park Zoo & Aquarium

'First Prize' Rose

'Freesia' Rose

Rose Garden & Pavilion
(Stanley Park)

John Church
Rose

Along with wild flowers and natural growth, Stanley Park has numerous carefully tended floral gardens. One of these, the famous Rose Gardens, delights visitors with its colour and delicate scents from mid-June to November.

Not far from the Rose Gardens is Stanley Park Pavilion, a rustic building nestled amongst tall trees and surrounded by a garden of ever changing colour.

The University of British Columbia and Queen Elizabeth Gardens also have spectacular rose gardens. Throughout Vancouver you can find roses spilling over fences or climbing over walls. No wonder the rose is Vancouver's official floral emblem.

21

Japanese
Dogwood
(Cornus kousa)

Flowering
Dogwood
(Cornus florida)

Flowering / Pacific
Dogwood
(Cornus nuttallii)

Although there are many beautiful varieties of dogwood, British Columbia has adopted the Pacific Dogwood as its official provincial flower. In springtime, the dogwood tree is covered with white bracts, just as though snow has fallen. The pink, more cultivated, Flowering Dogwood is also very popular in Vancouver, and so is the vase-shaped Japanese Dogwood which blooms for a month in early summer.

Lions Gate Bridge

The Lions Gate Bridge, at the north end of Stanley Park, connects the busy downtown traffic with the North Shore. It gets its name from "The Lions" – two nearby mountain peaks which resemble two lions guarding the city.

The Sea-Bus shuttles passengers across the Burrard Inlet, an interesting alternate connection between the busy downtown and North Shore.

Sea-Bus

The Marine Building
& detail of frieze

The Marine Building on Burrard and Hastings is
now over-shadowed by taller structures, but when it
opened in 1930 it was known as Vancouver's
"skyscraper". It is still a significant landmark not
only for its colourful history but also for its exquisite
detail. Intricate carvings of seahorses, pufferfish and
other marine life on the interior and exterior of the
building make it one of my favourites.

Rhododendron

Rhododendron simsii

opening buds

becomes woody stem

Rhododendrons, or "Rhodies" as they are affectionately called, provide Vancouver with a long season of brilliant colours. I drew these two varieties during late spring when they are at their best. Vancouver's peaty soil and moist growing climate provide excellent growing conditions for rhododendrons and azaleas which flourish throughout the city.

From a run-down skidrow to a revitalised shopping area for tourists and Vancouverites – Gastown is truly a remarkable transformation. Red brick streets, quaint alleys, ornate old buildings, unique street lights and hanging baskets add to the charm of this historic place.

Maple Tree Square

Marigold
Tagetes

Gassy Jack
Statue

Gastown originated in September 1867 when "Gassy" Jack Deighton, a talkative saloon owner, arrived by canoe from New Westminster. A community quickly grew around his new saloon. In 1885, under a large maple tree in the current Maple Tree Square, the founding fathers chose the name "Vancouver" for their city. The city was incorporated in 1886.

Nearby is a statue of "Gassy" Jack standing, of course, on a whiskey barrel.

Gastown Steam Clock

Detail of Lamp

At the corner of Water and Cambie Streets stands a large clock which is powered by steam from the heating system of nearby buildings. This unique clock, a popular tourist attraction, was dedicated to the citizens of Vancouver in 1977 in recognition of the restoration of Gastown.

During one of my strolls through Gastown in July, I happened upon these impatiens growing in Gaoler's Mews. This quaint, brick-lined alleyway is where the police once stabled their horses. Shady trees, flowerbeds, wrought iron lamps and railings, shops and restaurants, make this area one full of character.

Gaoler's Mews

Impatiens

Pansies/Viola

(Sweet Pea)

Lathyrus

(Perennial Pea)
—wild

colour ranges
pale-pink to bright rose

30

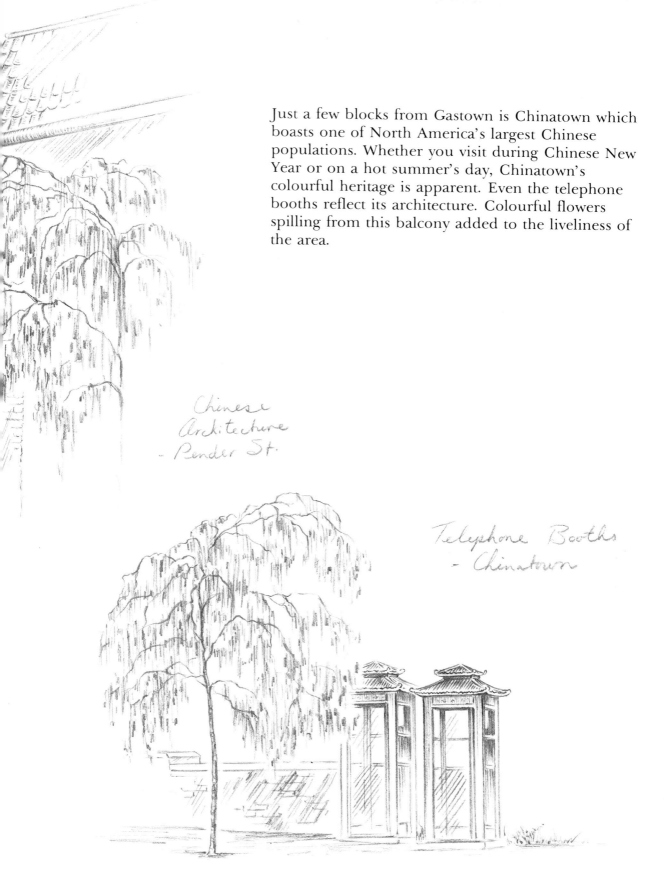

Just a few blocks from Gastown is Chinatown which boasts one of North America's largest Chinese populations. Whether you visit during Chinese New Year or on a hot summer's day, Chinatown's colourful heritage is apparent. Even the telephone booths reflect its architecture. Colourful flowers spilling from this balcony added to the liveliness of the area.

Chinese
Architecture
- Pender St.

Telephone Booths
- Chinatown

Fuchsia

False
Creek
(south side)

B.C. Place

False Creek
Marina

False Creek, a major industrial centre in the 1930's, is the site of Vancouver's urban redevelopment in the 1980's.

Fuchsia and lush plantlife grace entranceways to the modern townhomes on False Creek's south bank. Looking north, beyond the tranquil setting of moored sailboats, is the impressive B.C. Place Stadium and site of Expo 86, the world's fair.

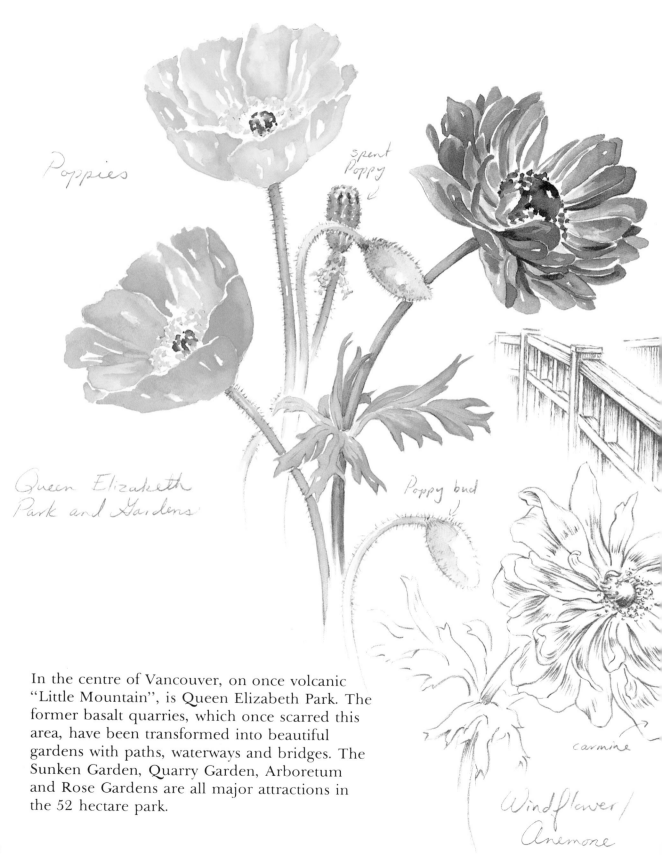

Poppies

spent Poppy

Queen Elizabeth Park and Gardens

Poppy bud

carmine

Windflower/ Anemone

In the centre of Vancouver, on once volcanic "Little Mountain", is Queen Elizabeth Park. The former basalt quarries, which once scarred this area, have been transformed into beautiful gardens with paths, waterways and bridges. The Sunken Garden, Quarry Garden, Arboretum and Rose Gardens are all major attractions in the 52 hectare park.

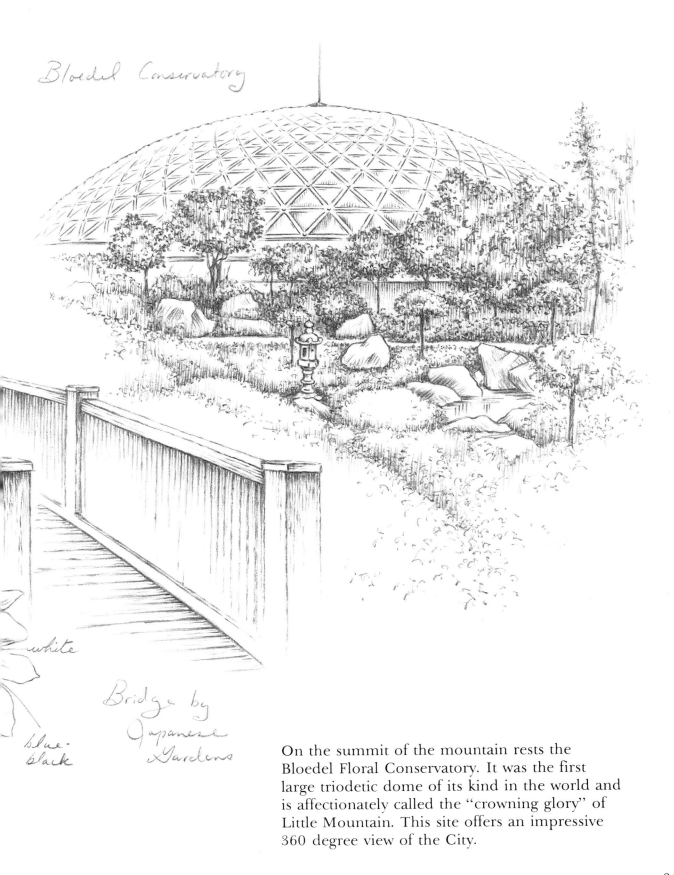

Bloedel Conservatory

white

blue-
black

Bridge by
Japanese
Gardens

On the summit of the mountain rests the
Bloedel Floral Conservatory. It was the first
large triodetic dome of its kind in the world and
is affectionately called the "crowning glory" of
Little Mountain. This site offers an impressive
360 degree view of the City.

Inside Bloedel Conservatory

Tropical plants, exotic flowers and several species of birds are housed within the special climate controlled environment of the Bloedel Floral Conservatory. Strolling around one passes through rain forests, the steamy tropics and an arid desert – all under one roof!

Euphorbia splendens

Agapanthus africanus

Granville Island
Public Market

Under Granville Street Bridge, where once stood derelict
factories and warehouses, is the thriving Granville Island. A
major attraction is the old-world atmosphere of the Public
Market where you can purchase everything from fresh seafood
to plants.

Burrard Bridge

Geranium, Ageratum & Marigold

Go round the back of Granville Island Public Market and you look over False Creek towards the downtown area. Part of this view takes in the Burrard Street Bridge, one of three bridges connecting the downtown peninsular with the south side of False Creek.

H. R. MacMillan
Planetarium

The H.R. MacMillan Planetarium, with its unique conical
dome and modern design, is a Vancouver landmark.
Located in Vanier Park, it is part of a large complex which
includes the Centennial Museum as well as many archival
and cultural facilities.

A large stainless steel crab, symbolic of nature's
dominance over human civilization, guards the entrance.

Vanier
Park

Begonia

Just outside the Planetarium the gardener was tending these wax begonias. It was a warm day in late July so I was delighted to find a trickling stream leading to the Maritime Museum.

Looking back towards the Planetarium I was able to capture this lovely setting of a graceful bridge and bowing trees with a rustic anchor in the foreground.

Shaughnessy Heights is the inspiration of the Canadian Pacific Railway which sold its landholdings in this area at the turn of the century. Shaughnessy gets its name from a C.P.R. president and many streets are named after officials of that company. My sketch is of McRae House, typical of the elegant homes in the area.

As I walked along the quiet streets of Shaughnessy and passed by the graceful manors, I took note of the many varieties of flowers – including these vibrant dahlias – which were blooming on the tranquil mid-August day.

McRae House – 'Hycroft'

Dahlia
- from garden in
Shaughnessy Heights

From summer through autumn, hydrangeas can be seen flowering all over Vancouver. The hues of these flowers range from powder blue to pink to deep mauve, depending upon the acidity of the soil in which they are grown.

Hydrangea

Shasta Daisy

Phlox

Tatlow Court

This sketch of Tatlow Court's garden apartments depicts some of the charm of Kitsilano. It literally overflows with all sorts of flowers and plants. Rows of majestic trees canopy many streets, and several streets are named after the trees growing along them.

Christ Church Cathedral

Chrysanthemum

Red-hot poker &
Snapdragon

I think the gardens of Vancouver are at their best from late August through to September. One of my favourite perennials, at this time of the year, is the snapdragon. As its name suggests, the flower resembles the snout of a dragon; pinching the sides forces the dragon's jaw open and, when released, they snap shut.

Now dwarfed by downtown office towers, Christ Church Cathedral is the oldest surviving church in Vancouver. Another heritage building, the Old Hastings Mill Store, is located in the more placid setting of Pioneer Park beside Jericho Beach. Now a museum, it is the oldest building in Vancouver.

Old Hastings Mill Store

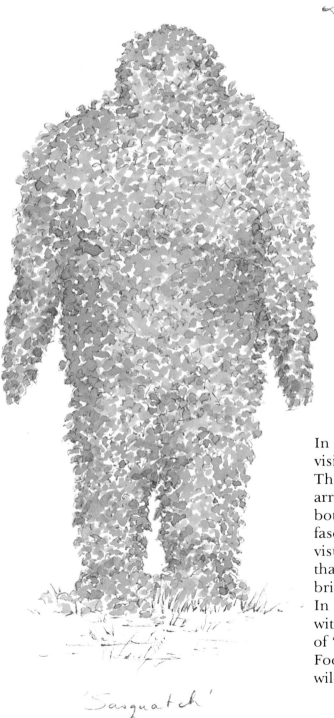

Van Dusen Botanical Garden

'Sasquatch'

In early October, my husband and I visited the Van Dusen Botanical Gardens. The plants in this 23 hectare garden are arranged by their geographical origin or botanical relationship and provide a fascinating learning experience. The visual impact of this scarlet sage was such that I felt compelled to record its brilliance of detail.

In the Children's Garden, I was delighted with the sculptured hedges including one of "Sasquatch" – the legendary "Big Foot" which, some say, roams the wilderness areas of Western Canada.

The Children's
Garden

Scarlet Sage

Bamboo

Vancouver's moderate climate
nurtures a variety of exotic plants
from other parts of the world.
Bamboo, pampas grass, yuccas, the
unusual Monkey Puzzle tree and
many more have all been adopted by
Vancouver's gardeners.

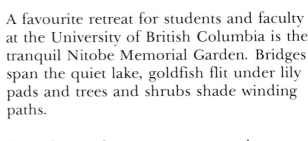

Nitobe Memorial Garden

A favourite retreat for students and faculty at the University of British Columbia is the tranquil Nitobe Memorial Garden. Bridges span the quiet lake, goldfish flit under lily pads and trees and shrubs shade winding paths.

Several stone lanterns are scattered throughout the Garden. I have drawn the yukimi or "snow view" lantern which is said to reveal its true beauty when covered with a light dusting of snow. The Garden is dedicated to the memory of Doctor Inazo Nitobe, an internationally known educator and landscape artist.

Totems - Museum of
Anthropology

52

Maple

Sumac

As well as by its majestic mountains, Vancouver is also
identified by its many artistic totems. These North West
Coast Indian totem poles, which I saw during a visit to the
University of British Columbia's Museum of
Anthropology, harmonize with the vibrant colours of an
Indian summer.

Point Atkinson

Lighthouse Park

One of my favourite areas for hiking is Lighthouse Park in West Vancouver. The trails take you through virgin forest with some of the tallest trees in the province. One trail leads to Point Atkinson where your reward is a lovely view of the lighthouse, the ocean and, in the distance, downtown Vancouver.

There are two suspension
bridges in the Vancouver area –
the largest at Lynn Creek and
the longest at Capilano Canyon.
However, not being one for
heights, I prefer this rustic and
stationary wooden bridge over
Lynn Creek's tumbling
waterfalls. I could not resist
painting these late roses.

Special displays are created throughout the year at the Park and Tilford Gardens in North Vancouver, but the gardens at Christmas are the most spectacular. Poinsettia and other flowers are protected by plastic domes and the Christmas lights transform the gardens into a Winter Wonderland. Truly Vancouver is a Garden.

Poinsettia

Brockton Point
Lighthouse
- Stanley Park

Raspberry
Blossoms

Vancouver's Untamed
Garden
(in June)

Ox-eye
Daisy

Fern